COLLECTED POEMS OF WAR & PEACE

BY
PETER HALL & JOHN CURTIS

This Book of Poems Is Dedicated
To The Memory
of
Edward Thomas, Poet.
Born 3rd March
1872
Died at Arras 9th April
1917

Contents

Wet Land In Gloster	6
Green Woodpecker	7
1914 - 2014	
Clematis	8
A Walk Back To	9
Grandad. July 2014	
to July 1916	
Ink	11
Nests	12
Pines and Church	13
Telegraph poles	14
The Sow	15
A Private of The Glosters	16
Dreams of Cotswold. 1916	
A Tribute to Ivor Gurney	17
Wendover	18
A Prayer In The Dark	19
Ypres 1917	
Light	20
Pools Night 1950	21
Rural Landscape After Stubbs	23
The Cornfield	25
A Walk In Autumn Rain	26
Summer 1914	28
General Orders 1915	29
Oak trees, so noble	30
Dandelion Days	31
Never Stole my Cattle	33
The Cure	34
For Tomorrow we Sleep	35
The Kingfisher	36
The Death of a Hero	38
Adlestrop 2015	39
Wendover Woods	40

The Green Man	41
Godspeed and thank you	43
Effigies	44
Undertones in War	46
Hill 60 - Messines Ridge	47
3:10 a.m. 7th June 1917	
Here along the gun line	49
Young Pretender	50
The Yew	52
Mute Swans Passing In The Night	53
Oxford 1949	
Waiting For The Kettle To Boil	54
The Master Butcher	56
Waiting To Go Over The Top 1915	58
Whilst the Sun sent its light	59
The Subaltern's Song	60
Seven Deadly Sins	61
Ancient Shadows	62
May	64
Through The Looking Glass	65
Images from the Front. 1916	
Upon his breast, a poppy grew	68
The Pike	69
Sheep in the Rain	71
A drama in front of small waves	72
Lice 1915	73
This is our England	74
Red-tailed Kite	75
Carrion Crow	77
The Grass in France	78
The Final Tempest	79
Robert Frost	80
By the dead pier-a man paused	82
The Legend of Old Bill	83
Quiet	85
Did death kiss your lips ever gently?	86

'The right of Peter Hall & John Curtis to be identified as authors of this book has been asserted in accordance with Section 77 of The Copyright, Designs & Patents Act 1988'

'All Rights Reserved'

Wet Land In Gloster

The wet land is dressed in beech
Clothed and polished with honeysuckle.
Ill at ease, with the falling rain
Gloucester grasps personality.
Intent to wipe away mulled damp
Breeze around, slip up Cotswold side
and rouses a day to play.

Now fair in the morning, strong streams
Break noisy through cloud. Commuting gulls,
all heady and foreign, hold fast to the plough
line.
A multitude of travellers
Broad shouldered and fleet
Wake farms who itch
with willing hands.

Indifferent lines
watch a carnival depart.
Past broken fence and badly cut sedge
to earn in wet fields.

PH

Green Woodpecker. 1914 - 2014

A green woodpecker taps an
Insistent message.
His black-clawed feet gripping the
Crusted bark of an oak tree.

His narrow head thrusts urgently,
Like the supple hips
Of a virile young lover
Between soft, welcoming thighs.

But the far-off ratatat
Reminds me of distant
Machine guns on Vimy Ridge
And the slaughter of lost youth.

JC

Clematis

The ivy-hung, beech wood lights the way to the gate.
With slick wet pockets of dusk
Full of woodland fluff.
A solid mark of foot prints.
Should guide me down
My pale-tint lanes.

I come here
To sip the persistence of English peace.
Note how brambles sit
in our very best seats.
And speak in tongues
to thick-set bands of nettle.

Our aspect of peace
Is this.
Clematis, with its flowers,
Of pink and blue and laced with
Lilac.
Daily fights
to flourish
in vast, green lawns of grass

PH

A Walk Back To Grandad. July 2014 to July 1916

On the soft green hillside stands
the dark rook swirled mass
of a tangled copse.
Scattered across the hollowed
fields are the small white
bolls of sheep, like fleas
on a green giant's arm.

Overhead the faint drone of
an aircraft, scratching
white tracks across the
deep blue porcelain sky.
The dusty, ochre lane
wanders like a drunken,
homeward bound yokel.

Before me, the plunging crest
of the ribbon roadway
falls invisible
to the lane's trough, then climbs
again to the next ridge.
In the far distance
a squat church tower.

There is a rapid, machine-gun stutter,
as a green wood-pecker in
the nearby copse, breaks the
warm and sultry silence.
Suddenly my Grandad is
young and spry again, struggling,
sweating and killing.

Charging with his bayonet,

alongside his khaki pals.
Across a century
echoes drift from the bloody
heights of Delville Wood
as the faint ghostly sounds of
ancient slaughter die away.

And Grandad is quiet in
his grave again.
Under the crab-apple trees.

JC

Ink

In time's libraries of books
Today is carefully set.
Close type;
Heavy
All tints and hues.

Leave editor at his desk.

The page of days
Shuts
With a candle puffed.

When flames of gold
Propose.

That ink, thick, rich and keening
will polish the slate of night.

                                                PH

Nests

Winter winds have raped the hedgerows,
stripping them of their cryptic greenery;
exposing nests invisible in Spring and Summer,
secreted in the snatching depths
of hawthorn and may.

Delicate wattle and daub bowls,
lined with thistledown and soft feathers,
plucked from a small bustling parent's
swelling, dappled breast.
Once crammed with seething pot-bellied
nestlings. Wide beaks agape.

Beaks yellow hinged, like the corners
of old men's mouths. Crowding the white-
flecked lip of the nest, begging paupers at the
dole hatch
of a mediaeval gate-house.
As harassed parents come and go.

Now askance, cockle-shell coracles
aground on a bank of spiny-thorned twigs
thin as sparrow's legs. Torn and ragged. Rifled
jewel
boxes, containing the wrinkled
ruby berries of hawthorn,

And small sherds of broken, arced shell.
Fragile reminders of pale turquoise eggs,
splashed with dark chocolate, lying in the
shallow and
swirled cup. Engendering a kind
of nascent Spring in me.

JC

Pines and Church

This picture would work best in oils.
Requiring detail
Not the vast wash of colour.
A gallery rich in pine
Picture sketched and line.
Our simple float of local notes which
Hang and claim the morning.
Like children upstairs.

Nursery tunes
Laugh and chip.
Place hands on top

Chiff-chaff is oldest.
Her half-tone song,
sits somewhere within needles.
There, silent, hardly of note
Woodland Sunday drifts.

Back to the pines
Bells draw weekend saints to church.
Pastel stone matching
Never old; the fake,
Mock-made and Sunday resplendent.

Rich window, trapper of stained light
Light our congregation.
Parades of hats and chaps,
With accents tremendous.
People of the County
God steps lightly here

PH

Telegraph poles

Walking the country lanes as a boy,
I would mark my dawdling progress
by my shoe-scraping passage between
those tall, dark sentinels, weeping
viscid, black treacle from their fissured,
and sun-baked ligneous hides.

Supporting liana looped overhead wires.
Apparently innocuous, a dwarf adder
sleeping beneath the shifting demerara
sands secreting sudden, shocking
death from the lightest, brushing touch.
Quiescent but deadly.

Near the peak of these pitch smeared masts,
grew a crop of heavy, white ceramic
bobbins. Barrels, mysterious
as Tibetan prayer-wheels.
Conduits of raw, monstrous power.
Dowsers. Electric shamans.

I would often stop and bend my head
to the sticky, tar-exuding timber.
Listening, spellbound, to the deep humming
of the pulsing poles. Like a distant
black swarm of angry honey bees far
away, rising from a rifled field of rape.

A swelling, primaeval resonance;
ivory chanters droning from the dank,
tangled rankness of the stinging, scourging
nettles.
Bearing the protean oscillation
of the expanding universe. Inchoate

faint echoes of the Big Bang.

											JC

The Sow

The full, fat belly of an upturned sow.
This hill, square, set at angle.
This nameless dale.
Gorse, twists high. Open and common

Home to strident Yellowhammer
He can sing till moon
Dazzling the plateau.

After-sunset
The gorse-yellow flowers strain
To match the heat of bird song.

Long, late feature, dropping beats
across the snare of our moon.

PH

A Private of The Glosters Dreams of Cotswold. 1916 - A Tribute to Ivor Gurney

Oh, that I might see
The lazy High Street again,
Moreton, all renewed,
Fresh, shining after rain.

And Chipping Campden's trees
In glowing Autumn hues;
Blockley under the moon,
Silvered with gleaming dews.

I last saw Bourton Hill
Against the sunset's rays,
And Blockley's clamorous bells
Coloured my childhood days.

The bright clustering stars
Above the twinkling Vale;
The smell of Autumn smoke,
The taste of Cotswold ale.

A soft burr of Cotswold talk
In cosy Cotswold inns,
Friendly skittle games
And crash of falling pins.

The scent of fresh baked loaves;
Quiet walks by quiet streams.
But this is not my home
And these are empty dreams.

                                          JC

Wendover

Snow fluffed hills; announce February.
Roman roads endless; bickering beech.
The Vale looks pants in wet bottoms.
Blanket of rooks. Now woke
since night was muted by movement.
Under Rothschild's red ridges
Couples kiss sleep goodbye.
Smiles soon yawn into daylight.

Tiny, slipper tiffs.
Teapots desperate, needy for work.
First toast! Shout loud for breakfast
Best dress quick
these gunboat clouds. Sinking in
could threaten a coup.
Or two.

PH

A Prayer In The Dark - Ypres 1917

A mad devil in the throttling night.
Tearing, shredding death passes
moaning like some hellish tram.
"Oh God, let this pass from me,
to fall on some other poor bugger
cowering in a premature grave....."

"If I come through this insanity,
on my oath, no more sweaty
fornication with the girls
at Madame Marie's ' Maison de joie'.
No more rich, dark looted wine from
the cellars of a shell-burst estaminet"

"I shall be good............
Until the next time"

JC

Light

Warm scent, drift on me.
From where
I know not.
In the aging daylight
each second is stretched
and sound seeks a stranger.

Strident and loud
A tale of sadness,
of warmth gone away.

Dancing light, leave on the hour glass.
Lost lover, you pass today.

                                                             PH

Pools Night 1950

That silence for the football results;
Intoned like Resistance shibboleths
Over the crackling, hissing airwaves.
Deep and sacred as the annual
Two minutes. Remembering those
Who never returned to do the Pools.

'Littlewoods', so liberal with spare forms which,
Never wasted, were torn, folded and shaped
Into slim paper spills. Tapers
To light pipes and hand-rolled cigarettes,
The gas cooker and the living room fire.
Crowding the brass shell case. Waiting,

Like white faced men, to go over the top.
The poetry of leagues and clubs,
Cadences of The Shipping Forecast.
A weekly war of attrition was waged
Against Chance. Draws, Wins, the odds
Ticked off with deadly concentration.

Grampy was already a winner
In the greatest wager of them all;
Surviving both the First and Second
Battles of The Somme and coming home
To tell the tale. Which he never did.
His only souvenirs were shell cases,

A machine gun bullet from Hill
Sixty, a brass tin of chocs. This a gift
From Queen Mary. Hard now and quite
Inedible. Untouched. Untasted.
Trench-foot topped this meagre list.
Black, bandaged feet until his dying day.

I think Gramp knew he'd never have a
Big Pools win; his life-time's luck was
Spent in the blood and mud of The
Western Front. It would be hubris
To expect more. He had seen hell
And endless horrors, but he never lost hope.

                                                        JC

Rural Landscape After Stubbs

Standing, patient, in the rain.
Sheltering beneath a horse-chestnut tree.
Faded green canvas cape draped
Across a broad velvet back,
Looped under her flaring tail.
Head bowed. Resting one hoof.
Biding her time.

At least the rain keeps the flies
Away from sensitive eyes and ears, while
The world is calm and silent
But for the 'Plip' 'Plip' of the
Fat, oily tear-drops falling
From wet, ganja shaped leaves.
A faint toll.

That great axe-head is empty,
Lost in a waking dream of ancestral
Plains, when, with no warning, a
Ripe conker, encased in it's
Green leathery barbed jerkin,
Drops on her plump peach
Of a rump.

Ancient instincts fire sleepy
Synapses. Her soft, brown eyes coil madly
Back into the deep, hollow
Sockets of her rearing head.
White as billiard balls. Wild,
And fearful. Staring globes
Of terror.

She already feels the deep,
Slashing talons in flinching hind-quarters.

The stinking breath at her throat
And in her flaring, satin
Nostrils. Screaming in primal
Panic she rears up,
Then falls back.

A conker lies on damp grass,
Its olive husk split and the white doe-skin
Of its inner sheath showing.
The varnished mahogany
Of the concealed nut revealed.
Trembling, the mare is still
And calm again.

Unscathed, she drifts back into
Somnolence and impassive ennui.
The last echo of her rending
Whinney fades into the soft,
Dripping tattoo of the last
Of the rain and all is
Tranquil once more.

JC

The Cornfield

The cornfield washes its hair
Against the beach of the hedge,
and the afternoon wind waves its fringes.
Straight, muddy paths
Cut the man-maize
Into blocks.
Half progress, half nature.

Back at the hedge,
The mechanical cut
Looks like a murderous brow.
Flailed and torn, this year's nest
holds no hope for fledgling.
Tattered drifts, on the barber's floor,
Waiting for a sweeper.

The youth on work experience.
Who sat on his tractor
like a gangling cowboy.
Hoping his ride is docile.

PH

A Walk In Autumn Rain

In the fields
The sheep lie like wet towels
Thrown on a sodden floor;
As if a giggling
Regiment of teenage girls
Had showered and left
For greener grass.

The raindrops
Fleck the sallow fleece, glinting
Like cut diamonds,
As narrow suede jaws
Move rhythmically, old men
Chewing green quids of
Tobbacco.

Impervious
To any discomfort or
Vexation. Wet wool
Being no different
Than dry to a sheep. A matted
Oilskin for these moist
And fruitful days.

The older wiser
Ewes have gathered like old women
Under the broad dark,
Dripping canopy
Of an aged, fissured oak tree.
Their incurious
Eyes following me.

The ancient footpath
Is a chocolate-brown smudge

Drawn hesitantly
Across the meadow
Toward the far line of hedgerow.
My boots slip and slide
Among black droppings.

The sheep continue
To chew, old eyes gazing on
The eternal fields.
Unnaturally
Quiet. A quiet broken only
By calls of crows and the
Soft patter of rain.

JC

Summer 1914

Good days for corn-fed mice.
Fat-cheeked, and sleek
They pirouette
Stalk high amongst the mess.
Whilst gentle, wheat-fields wash.
Across the wind, this harvest takes
and waits for lusty sons.
To scythe and clear, then stook and beer
Stack sheaves in autumn piles.

                                                       PH

General Orders 1915

The General mused as he toyed with his wine
In a borrowed Chateau ten miles from the line.

"The men need some action to keep on their toes;
Perhaps some trench raids ? We'll see how it goes."

His aide-de-camp smiled, gave a discreet cough;
As the General poured him more wine to quaff,

"Trench raids are all well and good, sir," he said,
"But men MUST be tempered if they're to be led."

"May I suggest a full frontal assault ?
And if it's a failure it won't be your fault."

"By Gad !" said the General, "That's just what we need !"
(In a stately Chateau, you don't see your men bleed.)

He rose and he nodded his fine martial head.
But because of those fools the men are all dead.

JC

Oak trees, so noble

The countryside was my surrogate
Green classrooms detain.
Listen boy. Stay late.
Let me explain,
Dovedale's song of soaring life.

Slip off your overcoat
Sit back, listen, in 3D sound.
Rasps of woodland bark.

Remember homespun evenings?
Teeth-broken walls, frame downstairs dips
Brave notes on a limestone canvas.
Hang off gates and see aloft,
The battleships of the peak.

And cheeky brooks, that natter late, then
bubble down ramshackle hips.
Dawdle here, confide and lie; within the
greenwood branches.
Pleasing breeze blow hours lost, with drawn old
Mr Jones.
Wisk away his spider scowl, and endless
drawing pin minutes.

                                                          PH

Dandelion Days

I remember lying in
Warm, scented pasture.
Buried in the secret jungle
Of a myriad wild flowers.
Blue, violet, pink, yellow and scarlet.
The haunt of jewelled beetles
And tiny, buff fray-winged moths.

The sun, burning over my head,
Searched like a questing
Hawk for me, recumbent in the
Margin of a great, dark ink-blot
Of shade, bleeding from a tall, majestic elm.
While golden talons of the
Sun-hawk, grasping, covetous,

With hungry persistence, again
And again, peeled the
Shrinking shadows from my tender
Limbs. Pushing me further under
The over-arching parasol of the
Cool, green canopy and broad,
Scuted belly of the giant elm.

The small bunch of yellow groundsel,
Which I had gathered
For my Gran's canary, Joey,
Drooped and wilted in the rising heat;
As the piquancy of vinegary
Blood-red sorrel leaves bit my tongue
And fat bumblebees droned nearby.

Green and blue metallic dung-flies
Settled on my sweating

Skin; while in the far blue distance,
A toy silver-grey, portly whale
Rose in the afternoon sky. A tiny
Gondola hung beneath it's swelling
Hide. A precarious roost.

Reaching the limit of it's earth-bound
Cable, the pygmy
Leviathan paused, swaying
Gently in the sun. To survey
The Lilliputian world below.
Then, magically, a handful
Of white floating dandelion seeds tumbling.

The distant parachutes fell, palely,
Like early snow-flakes.
Tardy, to the straining ground.
All that afternoon the barrage balloon
Rose and fell, tirelessly against
The turquoise sky. Releasing
It's apple-blossom cargo to the plucking breeze.

That enchanted afternoon lives on,
Like a distant echo,
In the forsaken lumber-room
Of my adult mind. Faded
And muted, but still evoking
The acetic flavour of wild
Sorrel on my naïve, artless tongue.

JC

Never Stole my Cattle

Often, I am dragged
to mills
of previous life.
Drip-days by waiting bus.
A blazered, standing line.

Often when I look
in cups
of morning lost.
See cricket day's sublime.
Contented-bubble time.

Always, if I'm asked
of tales,
An evening past.
Brave Hector's rolling tears.
Of ramparts, broken; lost.

Forever, I will shroud;
The sigh
of raining dawn.
Funerals of Troy,
and mournful, silent men.

However, I am cast
in days,
of earned respect.
Long days of routine lives,
But man of honour bound.

PH

The Cure

He crouched in the trench
Refusing to stir,
Trembling and shaking
Like an ill-treated cur.

The Colonel was told, said
"What's up with the fellow ?
Shell shock my arse !
The man's just plain yellow !"

A Court Martial will cure
Any soldier struck dumb.
Who shook and who wept
And who cried for his Mum.

"Cowardice in the face
Of the enemy" they said.
The poor bastard was done.
He was already dead.

But he was no coward,
No disgrace to the Army.
It was two years of hell
Which had driven him barmy.

He was just a sick boy
Who wished he'd never been born.
So they did what they could
Then they shot him at dawn.

JC

For Tomorrow we Sleep

Sentry nod, dark whispers
The cadence of routine.
As those here sleep
That weary sleep of war.
Blanket homes and picture love.
Glazed memories unwound.

The wrap of sleep-dead fatigue
The nodding symphony of days
Spent shells on the line.
The sleep of day walkers
The sleep of shift
The sleep of tomorrow

Sleep.
Sleep now.

                                                PH

The Kingfisher

Perched on his thin, white-streaked,
Arthritic branch,
Above the swift, curling water
Of this hidden stream.

A small scrap of a bird.
Brilliant, vivid
With colour, like a drop of oil,
Spreading across a pool.

Patient, persevering,
As are all anglers.
Watching the tiny, stirring shadows
In the limpid depths.

Suddenly a bright flash,
A soft, barely heard
Splash in the cool water. Swimming
Down to the stream bed.

Pygmy wings, jewelled with
Tiny pearls of clinging
Bubbles, as twisting he grasps the
Unsuspecting prey.

Dreaming, silver minnows are
Snatched from fluid sleep
And motionless, aqueous trance,
To feed his hungry brood.

He emerges shaking his
Gleaming, wet feathers;
A squirming, metallic stickleback
In his long black bill.

He is a creature of
Sky and water;
A sharp flicker of sunlit colour
In the sultry air.

He seems to have flown through
Freshly painted rainbows;
Stolen colours drying in the sun.
'Alkyon Pteroenta'.

                                                              JC

The Death of a Hero

Fades.
The hero, who did
as asked. He returned to
Places changed, as changed.
He saw things done, in others name,
And wept. His flame consumed, a shell
man who cried, faded- but forever named hero.

A square in a world full of round,
Never needed to cry until downwards pulled.
He never loved Jesus as much he should

Looking at a place, which just moved along.
Passing him now, forgetting to wave.
He stayed in his fame.

Are we different? Will we fade?
Or remember these times, our faces glow
whilst people forget.
With old, sad faces snug.
I loved this war, but peace is boring.

PH

Adlestrop 2015

The trains don't stop here any more.
No-one comes and no-one goes,
No-one sweeps the platform floor
And in the meadow Rape now grows.

There is no hiss of venting steam,
Just the wind along the line.
No passengers to homeward teem;
No scent of flowering wild woodbine.

No willows, willow-herb, just grass,
No meadowsweet to please the eye,
where once was gold, now only brass
Under the cloudlets in the sky.

You still might hear a blackbird sing,
Above the sound of passing cars,
But soon the birds are on the wing
And tourists crowd the public bars.

JC

Wendover Woods

The wet chalk slips under ash hangers
Leafless and frigid
bare pallor and skin.
A park-side path lines the pitch.
Sludge, sludge, brisk shakes.

Escaping dogs, howling recognition
Snaps and socks of mud.
Glorious, gnashing, Sunday.
Home dogs, wolf packed
all hands and random notes

Play out in woods,
Deaf, silent, asleep.
Pawning their beauty
Powder flushes of make up
Dip dusting brushes in green.

Hide dog-owned days and drape
sprung curtains of mesh.
Matt melodies of England.

Deep hedges, litter, leaf

Winter-walker lacks a vista
bar puddle-games of small ones.
But birth, new burst and flattery
Shift the eye line
Shift the angle of land
Shift the melancholy, muddy madness.

England is spring.

PH

The Green Man

As a boy I felt his shadowy
Presence in the silent
And brooding shade of dark
Spinneys.

His heart beat a soft insistent
Tattoo in my temples
And thudding eardrums. He
Watched me.

I often glimpsed his swift shape's flicker
In the corner of my
Dazzled eyes. As one with the
Dappled leaves.

I sometimes spied his leaf-bound face
Among the stirring leaves,
Grinning down on me from
Squat, broad oaks.

I caught his green-nettle breath. A sharp
Animal musk filling my
Thrilled nostrils, freezing my
Hot blood.

I heard his wry, dry chuckle echo
In the whispering wind,
Rustling the fan-vaulted
Canopy.

He is the most ancient of the old
Gods; has haunted the deep
Woodlands and the lonely,
Blind copse,

Since before the building of Stonehenge.
His names are legion but
I know him as The Green Man.
The Watcher.

He was in the sacred groves of Attic
Greece, the endless forests
Of ancient Germany.
He endures.

He was biding in the glaucus dusk
Of Wittenham Clumps; his
Malachite eyes prickling
My icy spine.

The new life that rises each season
From the land's travail is
Of his engendering.
His green sap.

He is the force that drives the green spikes
Through the moist, dark fertile soil;
The golden pulse that swells
The barley.

JC

Godspeed and thank you

Thanks for the stars.
A great city
Happy in its image.
God speed, and thank you.
Back home I go.
Couples have an evening close

Rolling smiles and sleepy
Heads. The stars delight.
Reflections in the life
of a shuffling train.
Tracks open electric doors.

I rise, and see keen
February's disappointment
with the warm, quickening,
arrival
of singing spring. She

Dumps snow. Sullen branches
Whisper.
So snow, cling, shush.

Off home, dead slow
The Roman road to Tring.
A fox path wary

Thanks for the stars.
I live here now.
Off home, I go

PH

Effigies

Was there ever tender love between them ?
I mean when warm flesh clothed their ochre bones.
Long before these stone euphemisms
were laid to rest upon this uncreased marble bed ?

He in his sculpted armour, mailed hands pressed
together like a child at prayer. His feet,
in stone winkle-pickers, segmented like
petrified armadillos, curl over his lap-dog.

Legs tightly crossed, like a man severely
burdened with a distressingly full bladder;
yet stoic in his endless discomfort
as would befit one who fought at bloody Crecy field.

A chain-mail balaclava frames the
pale, gracile features beneath his pointed helm.
She lies rigid beside him, thinking of England.
Her gaze fixed on the fan-vaulted roof above her head.

Has she lain here for seven hundred years
Dreading his cold marble hand upon her
Ivory thigh ? Her hands fast in fervent prayer.
"Oh God, 'tis not Friday night, no droit du seigneur !"

Tiny chips and abrasions, the vandalism of
time; that greatest of iconoclasts, have bruised them

both. Accumulating like psoriasis through the
creeping centuries. And still they lie here
unmoved.

They must continue their unchanging deceit;
so that the common people shall never know
the
truth of this convenient marriage; contracted
for
family power. In life, colder than this haughty
tomb.

                                        JC

Undertones in War

The long sap seeped under pollards
recently scorched in fire.
On the frill of the crater,
a parapet pulverised,
by long drops on each side.
And a scrape is pulled from the mess.
Now home to a Vickers
Stuttering
Unhappy messages to Old Willie.
Hated
King of all Prussians.

Worthy men lugged timber
to fix a sap. Within the pollards
Men hammered. Vickers stuttered.
Muffled, and moving as drunkards
Sappers diced over duck-boards.
Worn, muddy boots in darkness.
Mud, always this mud.

In April rain, so drenching
it hid the weft of rolling smoke. Dirty, dank
and dangerous.
And the long sap, seeped onwards under
pollards.

Always, to sound of a Vickers
Stuttering.

PH

Hill 60 - Messines Ridge - 3:10 a.m. 7th June 1917

Scrabbling like albino moles beneath
the tortured Flanders fields,
hunched low, sweating,
snowblind in the
narrow earth. Candle-light reflecting
dazzling points from the
white chalk walls of
the creeping, cramping tunnel.

Stripped to the waist in utter silence,
broken only by
the muffled blows of
short-handled picks.
Advancing like white-powdered snails, mute,
bootless, whispering
like men in church.
Freezing at the slightest sound.

Each dry-mouthed Tommy, haunted by the
spectre of Hun counter-mines,
trying to still
his rasping breath.
Every tenter-hook shift with one
foot in life, the other
in the damp grave.
A sort of purgatory.

Daily they played a noiseless Russian
roulette, waiting for the
hammer to fall
on a full chamber.
Each Sapper, once a miner, had crawled
like earth-worms in brutal

coal fields; emerging
at dusk, black as Mummers.

Now, weary men exit the sap-trench like
white ants, chalk-dusted
human termites in
the French predawn.
Soon the abused earth will rise and roar,
a fleeting sugarloaf mountain,
erasing ten thousand men.
Apocalypse at three ten a.m.

JC

Here along the gun line

There will be fifty, little deaths today.
Here, in front of the gun-line.
Fifty, little deaths
Here on the gorse.
Not a single one will be clean.

Old England entertains herself.
Hear her bangs and beats.
The beat-bang, bloody shoot.
Listen to the larks,
Here along the gun-line.

The gun-line moves;
To a different hill.
And the little murders continue.
Here on the gun-line, there is money made.
Place bets
On, fifty little deaths.

                                        PH

Young Pretender

Some middle class bitch
stuck an envelope in his
childish, grubby hand.
A big boy for his age
but only thirteen.

He opened it in
the whining tram. Love letter ?
No, more a hate letter.
A single white feather
and a spiky note.

"Why aren't you at the Front ?
Are you a girl ? A coward ? "
He dared not look up, avoided
the other passenger's eyes.
The woman was gone.

Next day, playing truant
for the last time, he signed
his young life away.
No-one noticed he had aged
five years since yesterday.

His uniform fitted.
What more do you bloody want ?
His rifle was bigger
than he was, but men were often
shorter then. He didn't shave.

The men tried to look
after him. They knew the
score. But you can't protect
a beardless boy from a sniper

who couldn't know that
he was out of season.

JC

The Yew

The long line of the lane, drew its business
from a landscape of deep trees.
The bands of hornbeam, holding canopies
Statuesque.
Laagered by cream stone, the manor church
Built its memories

On silent air. Twinned with a headstrong yew,
White-wood and split by centuries.
It slept in Sunday stillness.

Briefly perturbed, by well-dressed patrons
The nods and winks of the County set.
With platitudes and stories of news
Menu's exchanged and then, in pews
The downward slump into Brahms.
Light inside, was golden and right
With first, gay rays, alighting on Jesus.
Touching briefly, a toothy vicar
Lecturing brightly, on how unsightly, the
current collection was.

Yew had known the old gods,
When angles of land sat different.
When the rich, warred on horses, and
ploughmen
Broke hands on harrows.

Protected short lives, constructs of weather
Clever men looked to war.
And pulling up their ploughman
Rode down the same, long lane
To do their bloody business.

PH

Mute Swans Passing In The Night - Oxford 1949

When I first heard the faint, rhythmic
Wheezing of their approach,
I leapt from my bed,
Running to the tiny window
Under the eaves.

Then I saw them, their serpentine
Necks swaying in perfect
Time with the leisurely
Beating of their ivory wings.
Crying like lost souls.

These pale triremes, glided across
The tumid face of the
Lambent moon, floating
Through the ragged, silver-stained clouds;
Soft, downy breasts lustrous.

Then, as the vox humana of
Their passing faded in
The distance, the night was
Usurped by the mundane clinking
Of the nearby shunting sheds.

JC

Waiting For The Kettle To Boil

Have you noticed how the early
Morning, soon after the
Dawn, smells like fresh washing on the
Line ? Just when the new day
Is stretching it's arms and yawning
Like a cat ?

Making the first, best pot of tea
Of the morning; scooping
Up the dry, mocha brown granules
Of curled leaf into a
Dark mound in the bowl of the
Old caddie spoon,

I found myself thinking of the
Scattered rows of toiling
Brown women in bright saris, like
Florid butterflies,,
Moving between the lines of bushes
On the green Assam hills.

Their glossy black hair parted and
Scraped back into thick
Braided tails, echoing the woven
Wicker baskets on their
Backs. Then the kettle boiled and I
Filled the waiting pot.

It was early, four-forty-five am.,
And from the garden I
Heard the sharp, urgent, metallic
'Chak-chak' of an indignant
Blackbird amid the stuttered calls
Of startled pigeons.

"It's the sodding cat !" I thought
Wearily. I knew it
Was she. Prowling. Savage feline
Thoughts boiling in her pretty,
Narrow head. Thoughts of bloody
Carnage. Of torn flesh.

I know her technique; her modus
Operandi. She feigns
Bored indifference to the rising
Volume of chittering
Calls. But her twitching tail tells quite
A different story.

And, of course, later on the
Flag-stones I find the plump,
Feathered corpse. Yellow rimmed eye slits
Closed as if sleeping. A
Few downy feathers stirring in
The breeze. A tiny, dark
Garnet of blood, like a gift, adorns
Her surprised, half-open beak.

                                              JC

The Master Butcher

Daily,
Master Butcher here
A gay order "pipe to all hands".
Efficient despatch of wet pigs.

Pigs with whiskers
Pigs with lop-snouts
Pigs with one eye
Pigs with one ear
All brought here
All died.
Here.

Murders by the pig mallet.
Like the devil's pendulum
It swings above the pits.
Lusty swipes with a lump of lead.
Whack.
Lusty swipes with a lump
Whack.
Lusty swipes.
WHACK.

Master Butcher has a sharp knife.
Lick the throats of the miserable sows.
Leave a gargling froth.

I see the pigs.
Faces smashed.
I see the pigs.
Trophy ears.
I see the pigs.
Trotters hacked and lost.
I see the pigs.

I see the pigs.

                                        PH

Waiting To Go Over The Top
1915

It is an awful thing
to see men in terror of the dawn,
strong placid men who,
plodding, followed plough and sweating team.

Men whose dearest wish
now is that they were never born,
As fond memories
of Cotswold hills fade in the sun's first gleam.

Each fleeting second
seems now a secret precious breath,
slipping through clenched lungs,
until that bloody pigsqueal whistle-blow.

Here white-faced pals teeter
on the brink of chattering tearing death
and fixed bayonets
reflect a last Woodbine's cherry glow.

Then the ungainly
scramble across the trench's crumbling brink,
a delicate step
over strands of tangled thorned barbed wire.

Advance in line toward
machine-guns and choking cordite stink.
To fall like sickled wheat,
Cut down in swathes by scything Jerry fire.

JC

Whilst the Sun sent its light

The sun was breaking through the top-gallants
Grading light
Etchings of fine sand, a jar,
From days of haze and shimmer.

Long drawn evenings, on set-me-free beaches
When toes were scented wet.
Stumps drawn and wickets left
For a Cornish sea to eat.

That final amble,
Up cork- failing cliffs
The call of the sea-birds
This book-time hour
Spent doing nowt
When moon and tide were wide.

PH

The Subaltern's Song

They say the guns drive sane men mad;
But only those of lower class.
In posh Chateau it's not so bad,
I've never known it break a glass.

The men make TOO much of the thing,
They're safe and cosy in a trench.
Why, sometimes you can hear birds sing !
Or so I'm told by General French.

I GRANT you men ARE sometimes lost;
Odd shells and bullets, things like that.
But that's the calculated cost.
It's merely martial tit for tat.

In war some men are BOUND to die;
It is the nature of the Art,
It's not for THEM to question why.
Here at H.Q. we play OUR part.

We rack our brains over our wine
And stroll the gardens making plans.
I'd LOVE to be in the front line
To have a crack at Fritz or Hans.

But I was born to be a toff,
We don't do filth and mud and stench.
A garden bonfire makes ME cough.
They don't dress for dinner in a trench.

JC

Seven Deadly Sins

This sunburn scrap of weathered life,
Is standing before HIS light.
" Before you're issued angels wings,
Be free from listed sins."

Did you live blame - free life?
Nor present with back-straight pride?
Expose the myth of Spartan might?
Offer lives bereft of pain?

Nay, triumph bold, whilst whispered slaves,
proclaim the glorious deed.
Take nothing from a neighbour's house.
But, travel paths to peace.

Finally, dear son of Mars, whilst marching off
to war.
Did you always, pause, stop and think,
And only ever fight for right?

                                                       PH

Ancient Shadows

There was always a prickling, nettle-sharp magic
which seemed to lurk in the depth of a whispering copse;
a tight, electric excitement. A cuckoo egg
in my arid throat.

I knew he was there, always fleeting. A quick,
flickering peripheral movement in the crowding
trees. His neat, sharp hooves and shaggy thighs brushing
the cool, damp undergrowth.

A lean, sardonic face glimpsed among the dappled
leaf-screen. Was it him or the pattern of sunlight
playing across the shifting, emerald back-cloth
of tangled bocage ?

Like a saturnine Uncle Sam, he winked and grinned
for a breathless moment from the bright, sequined,
lacy tapestry of a beech grove; ridged amber horns
coiled like ammonites.

Sometimes I thought I caught the faint piping of an
ancient syrinx. Was he sitting cross-legged on
a mossy rock ? Or maybe I had heard only
a harmony of birds.

It must be over sixty years since those brief encounters.
Profound and disquieting. Yet transcendent.
I know him still, ubiquitous and fecund.
The great begetter.

You will find him in the sprouting seed, the swelling
fruit and the fresh green blur of Springtime. He is the
driving force. Were I to return tomorrow to my youth, he would be there.

                                                              JC

May

It was a shady May evening.
I pause at the nick of the path.
Gate yawing and half-asleep
Listen to the nod of nature.
Within bracken, larks were low
Peregrines had returning wind.
Looking ahead, the path tacked
Up through hangers,
With their bones of pine.
Undergrowth trimmed and kicked aside

By forest men and ruddy desire.
Wide line of heavers, chipping to a rhythm,
Retreat the woodland, like a lazy hem.

Spy new lights, cross old margins.
I moved from the gate, past elms and chestnut
Crunching on last, low fruit
Setting my pack, to arrow for home.
In shady May
In any May
Who does not love England?

PH

Through The Looking Glass - Images from the Front. 1916

1.
Predators.

The bored Tommy
squinted at the hovering hawk
in the empty sky,
watched its falling swoop
from infinity to earth.

The Hun sniper
held his breath and squeezed the trigger
of his Mauser rifle.
As one the pigeon
and the man fell from earth into infinity.

2.
Comradeship.

Struggling, as he did on the farm,
with a bushel of barley on his broad back,
The big, ponderous private
staggers through the muddy trench
carrying his mate's dead weight
to the bloody, sobbing
dressing station.

Strained peasant face scowling
up at the intrusive lens, his pal's dark blood
soaking through his coarse khaki tunic.
Beloved mate. Always cheerful,
always shared the last Woodbine.
The sour taste of hatred

in his dry mouth.

3.
Time Off.

Men, stripped to the waist,
pick the lice from the seams
of their tick-stained shirts.
They lean forward, intent,
their thumbnails red and sticky.
Behind them close-wattled panels
hold back the clotted earth.

A couple of Tommies squat
over a liberated and drunken
cast iron stove,
slowly subsiding into the mud.
Slender, rusting chimney
like that of a Clyde Puffer
listing in the sea breeze.

A mate, holding his Lee-Enfield
against his side with long
sword bayonet fixed,
leans a nonchalant arm against
the sagging, sand-bagged parapet
of the narrow trench.
Relaxed but vigilant.

He peers through a rifle slit
across no-man's-land toward
the German front line.
His Boche counterpart
stares back at him.
Neither knowing that

Tomorrow both will be dead.

									JC

Upon his breast, a poppy grew

Upon his breast a poppy grew
Its petals darken slowly

Within his pack a letter read
Soft lilt to night-time candle

Outside this life his children grow
Lost in Flanders never know

That on his breast a poppy grew
And petals stained the khaki

PH

The Pike

He lies beneath the dark, silent shelf
Among the ribboned
Olive pondweed.
Floats like a sunken branch. Still, unmoving,
Except for a slight
Pectoral scull.
Keeping station.

His tiger body and powerful,
Undershot shovel
Of a jaw,
Cruel and arrogant, hidden in
Green shadows, await
The pink-tinged roach
And plump chub.

Stony, basilisk eyes watch minnows and
The serrated, red-
Bellied silver,
Stickleback, scudding in harmony
Through the sun-dappled
Shallows. Living by
This dark lord's leave.

In his cold mind's swart depths, some are marked
Already for the
Gathering.
They dart and freeze and dart again. Blithe
And unaware
Of their imminent
Demise. So close.

As small children released from irksome

Bondage. Playing on the
Slender, raw edge
Of infinity, while the steel spring
Of his scaly,
Narrow body is set.
A baited trap.

When it comes, the thrashing explosion
Of bubbling, whirling
Quick-silver
Water is sudden, shocking and over.
Tumbling, jewel-like scales
Sink to the turbid stream-bed,
Glinting like pearls.
.
Carnage wrought, the scattering, bright shoals
Coalesce again;
Unmindful
Of such recent death and sacrifice.
The fury past.
Then he is still again.
Droit de Seigneur.

                                                           JC

Sheep in the Rain

Fleece heavy with rain, some stand, heads
down,
Grazing on the sodden grass.
Others lie, jaws moving from side to side.
Silently ruminating.

What is moving through their sleepy minds.
The odour and taste of grass,
The irritating trial of flies;
The excited sporting of lambs ?

Lambs, which in the fresh-born joy of life,
Run and leap, kicking hind legs
Out, like young colts. Tremulously bleating,
Clamorous. Calling to each other.

Now and again, one will climb upon
It's supine mother's back, like
A leggy, woolly Cortez. Silent
Upon a peak in Darien.

I never tire of sheep. They are a
Tough and tolerant creature.
Their lives constrained by the endless
Cycle of conception and birth.

JC

A Drama in Front of Small Waves

I listen to the drama of small waves
The rhythm of an off-shore wind
The beat, soft-soft, in the water
The foam that startles walkers
And understand.
Happy is the man who walks on a beach
without the need to drown.

I listen to the speech of the dunlin
The angst of electric waves
The walkers, lonely, who look for a silence
The rhythm of the off-shore wind
And understand.
Unhappy is the man, alone on a beach
without the need to drown

PH

Lice 1915

A fat stub of candle,
more ivory than white.
Sooty flame trembling;
advancing slowly along
the seams of khaki shirts
and breeches.

The little bastards that
escape the scorching heat
are cracked between thick
and blackened thumbnails, smeared dark
crimson by borrowed
Tommy blood.

And it doesn't matter
how many of the tiny
sods you kill, you'll be
lousy again by tomorrow.
The maddening wee
buggers will be back.

But its a pleasant
way of passing a
quiet hour or two.
Between the striding
of the guns.

Stalking the trench seam
with sound beyond sound,
seething, searing flame
and crushing red hot
Hun shrapnel.

JC

This is our England

Slumped sodden, in an igloo of an Oxfam coat,
Is the crack-faced man and his faithful friend.
Happy in his anguish, he trembles and asks
for silver.
Flea-raw dog, with worrying eye, sings along.
Contracts to stay together. Despise the weather.
This is their life.
England.

The sneering day-time rush.
No pause for silver or the float of a note.
Stand-by for the Sally Army
All bosoms and bows. No tambourines.
Just welcome crutch and a chance of tea.
You see,
God works in his own way.
Today.

And in our England,
A black-frocked, cheery smile
Is your actual Jesus.
Jesus.
This is our England.

PH

Red-tailed Kite

Stoic all seeing
Nemesis.
Mewing watchful,
Surveying waiting fields.

Feathered fingers flexing,
Stirring the
Frigid air. Still,
Quiescent and weightless.

Dreams of carnage lie
Like hot coals
In his neat head.
Horus eyed, arc beaked.

Far below, a mouse,
Unconscious
Of fast approaching
Death, takes his final meal.

Plummeting from the blind,
Blue sky. A
Thunderbolt, fireball,
Bent on destruction.

Iron taloned, barbed
Feet breaking
The plump, warm body
Of his squealing prey.

Another hunter plans
A new life
For this sickleheaded
Killer. Blind caparisoned,

In eyeless leather
And plumed cap.
With ringing jesses,
Lobe-belled and bright tasselled.

To kill at a master's
Whim. His raw
Nature tamed and
Controlled. A feathered weapon.

A partnership of
Blood. Old as
The rise of man;
An ancient alliance.

JC

Carrion Crow

His gait is that of a drunken sailor,
belly full of carrion.
He has a beak like an obsidian anvil;
a thing of crushing power.
His polished, lapidary eye,
Regards me with indifference.

His handsome black head and sable plumage,
glint purple, oil on water
in the glancing morning sun. Regarding me without
apprehension, picking like a
gourmande at the broken pheasant.
Bored, he hops heavily to the verge.

There is no fear in his black button eyes.
Just cold calculation.
He knows me. This lonely lane is his dining place
And my morning walk, we respect
each other's privacy. I call him
'Blackwing'. He has no interest in my name.

                                                                  JC

The grass in France

They say we own the fine grass in France.
Perfect meadows, cross stones
which point to lawns in Belgium.

Once soil was bare as bones,
We farmed it. And now
our grass stands sturdy.
Stiff against the shells of time
Dark rolling vales surround us.

We own the finest grass in France.

PH

The Final Tempest

Rain, wild and lashing,
Break against the hard side.
It taps out slow solitude.
A bugle-recall of hot days
Great days.

Now, listen to the night-owls
The shuffling of badgers
The shriek of rabbit and fox.

You have no joy
For raw, lashing, life
Of green.

Just bitterness of an old age.
That vinegar of soul.
A spiteful anger, embalmed.
A life of stiffness.

The ghoul of night.
The stink fills your nostrils.
Helpless are you now.
This breaking tempest,
Is your last, good friend.

          PH

Robert Frost

The wayward billow
Of a forelock,
Capping the broad forehead
Rising like a granite bluff,
Is barely contained.

His deep-set eyes gaze
From a calm and
Stoic face. The face of
A New England dirt farmer.
Self-possessed and grave.

The broad 'A' of far-off
Sussex, carried
To the green hills and farms
Of rural New Hampshire, shaped
This poet's voice.

He knew how a firm,
New-plucked apple
Felt, cupped in a calloused
Hand. Fresh from the burdened tree.
It's sharp, clear smell.

He heard the soft sigh
Of the sweeping
Scythe through the ripe scented
Corn, in the morning's pressing heat.
The rising dust.

He knew the austere
And tragic truths
Which lay behind the bright,
Lush, fertile fields and woodlands

Of New England.

His practiced hands set
The slicing plough ;
Gripped the time-worn hickory
Pole of the sharp, probing hoe.
Tilled the rich soil.

He was a man, who,
While rooted deep
In the earth of his native
State, sowed transcendence in the
Minds of all men.

As a poet he
Saw, held in the
Mundane, a sudden and
Extraordinary glow
Of dazzling wonder.

JC

By the Dead Pier-a Man Paused

Here on a damp watercolour
Black spot gulls wrestle breakfast.
A Dutch landscape of a painting.

Along the shoreline, early risers shout hoarse
against grey lined waves. Moan; moan
the mourning beat of the wash.

Look for the lost. Those wrapped and
temporary absent,
from the blown words of a harridan.
Alone with solitary thoughts.
Avoid the brown stains of life at sea.
The long bored member of the hollow,
Walks the altar of sand.

Look for him. In his cord-sensible coat
Collar upright to upturn spirals
Deflecting sandpaper wasps.
Hunt for a break- just a single gap.
To pause, for an hour alone,
With new verse.
Dog worn and crumpled

Fingers pink and clumsy.
Halt, looking for meter,
But spy, spy, for odd signs of a tail.

By the pile of a dead pier; shelter,
Another page turned.
But the new verse labours.
This rhythm is false.   PH

The Legend of Old Bill.

Ol' Bill was never one to lose 'is 'ead
Just because 'is mates were dead.
'E'd just chew 'is Bully Beef,
Suckin' the trench dust from 'is teef.

Bill wuz British through an' through,
'E'd not let whiz-bangs spoil 'is brew.
'Is black pipe pierced 'is walrus 'tache;
Ignorin' Big Bertha's loud heavy crash.

'E was unmoved by mud and stench,
'E left 'isterics to the French,
To clear the lice out of 'is kit
'E always kept a candle lit.

A piece of corrugated iron,
Some duck-boards for 'im to lie on,
A bit 'o' peace an' quiet from Fritz
An' Bill's dugout wuz The Ritz.

If fresh green troops complained,
Bill told 'em in a voice real pained,
"If you knows some better 'ole,
Go to it ! " ('E could be reel droll !)

Bill 'oarded baccy like a miser,
'E wished a pox upon the Kaiser.
There weren't much could make 'im fret,
'E wuz a Regular Ol' Sweat,

'E sometimes wrote 'ome to 'is Missis;
The Censor blanked 'is love 'n kisses.
'E never told 'er where 'e wuz,
'E never knew 'imself becuz,

The Top Brass in their French Chateau
Saw no cause to let 'im know.
To them Bill was just another pawn
And 'ad been since 'e wuz born.

A Moanin' Minnie over'ead
Wouldn't git 'im orf 'is bed,
Bill took 'is shut-eye where 'e might
Whether it be day or night.

The army wuz 'is mum an' dad;
The only 'ome 'e ever 'ad.
It fed 'im. clothed 'im, paid 'im too.
(Though it wuz sometimes overdoo.)

A veteran of the B.E.F.,
Constant shelling sent 'im deaf.
An 'Old Contempible' was 'e,
E'd sell 'is soul for army tea.

E'd raise an eyebrow at a shell
An' wish the 'un to " soddin' 'ell."
'E always made poor Tommies grin,
Which eased the 'ell that they wuz in.

                                                         JC

Quiet

Silence sits in my world
and I embrace it.
It plays along strong corridors
where varnished floors can glide.
Hold my feet with lightest touch
and keep my days upright.

Silence sits in my world
and I seek it.
To fold alone, the wasted time,
and crush my modern life.
But hope I am remembered
and held in some esteem.

Silence sits in my world
and I miss it.
Walk alone without a friend
and set the memories right.
To sense the night, so far and still,
and bring this calm to sleep.

Silence sits in my world
and I embrace it.
To age listless, by its pool,
and watch the moon night pale.
Grasp its splendour, day by day,
and walk again with friends.

PH

Did Death Kiss your Lips ever Gently?

Did death kiss your lips ever gently?
Did you enter the night unknown?
Go, well rested, set sail alone
as dark lamps slowly burn

Did death kiss your lips ever gently?
Did you watch as your lover cried?
And, sobbing slowly, accept that life
is worth the grief inside

Did death kiss your lips ever gently?
Or leave you broke with pain?
Did you cry whilst others struggled?
And hope for a miracle, pray.

PH

Index of First Lines

A fat stub of candle	73
A green woodpecker taps	7
A mad devil in the throttling night	19
As a boy I felt his shadowy Presence	41
Daily, Master Butcher here	56
Did death kiss your lips ever gently?	86
Fades. The hero, who did as asked	38
Fleece heavy with rain, some stand, heads down	71
Good days for corn-fed mice	28
Have you noticed how the early Morning	54
He crouched in the trench Refusing to stir	34
He lies beneath the dark, silent shelf	69
Here, against a damp watercolour, black spot gulls,	82
His gait is that of a drunken sailor	77
I listen to the drama of small waves	72
I remember lying in warm, scented pasture	31
In the fields the sheep lie like wet towels	26
In time's libraries of books	11
It is an awful thing	58
It was a shady May evening	64
Often, I am dragged to mills	33
Oh, that I might see	17
Ol' Bill was never one to lose 'is 'ead	83
On the soft green hillside stands	9
Perched on his thin, white-streaked,	36
Rain, wild and lashing	79
Scrabbling like albino moles beneath	47

Sentry nod, dark whispers	35
Silence sits in my world and I embrace it	85
Slumped sodden, in an igloo of an Oxfam coat	74
Snow fluffed hills. Announce February	18
Some middle class bitch	50
Standing, patient, in the rain	23
Stoic all seeing	75
Thanks for the stars	43
That silence for the football results	21
The bored Tommy squinted at the hovering hawk	65
The cornfield washed its hair against the beach of the hedge	25
The countryside was my surrogate	30
The full, fat belly of an upturned sow	16
The, ivy-hung, beech wood	8
The General mused as he toyed with his wine	29
The long line of the lane, drew its business	52
The long sap seeped under pollards	46
The sun was breaking through the top-gallants	59
The trains don't stop here any more	39
The wayward billow Of a forelock	80
The wet chalk slips under ash hangers	40
There was always a prickling, nettle-sharp magic	62
There will be fifty, little deaths today	49
They say the guns drive sane men mad	60
They say we own, the fine grass in France	78
This picture would work best in oils	13

This sunburn scrap of weathered life	61
Upon his breast a poppy grew	68
Walking the country lanes as a boy	14
Was there ever tender love between them ?	44
Wastes of seed heads	20
When I first heard the faint, rhythmic Wheezing	53
The wet land is dressed in beech	6
Winter winds have raped the hedgerows	12

Printed in Great Britain
by Amazon.co.uk, Ltd.,
Marston Gate.